This book belongs to:

_____

It was given to me by:

_____

On:

_____

Print ISBN 978-1-62836-892-5

eBook Editions:
Adobe Digital Edition (.epub) 978-1-63058-578-5
Kindle and MobiPocket Edition (.prc) 978-1-63058-579-2

Published by Barbour Books, an imprint of Barbour Publishing, Inc., P. O. Box 719, Uhrichsville, Ohio 44683, www.barbourbooks.com

Our mission is to publish and distribute inspirational products offering exceptional value and biblical encouragement to the masses.

Member of the
Evangelical Christian
Publishers Association

Printed in the United States of America.
04687 0814 VP

Christmas Prayers
for Bedtime

JEAN FISCHER
ILLUSTRATED BY **DAVID MILES**

BARBOUR
PUBLISHING

Contents

God's Promise

Therefore the Lord himself shall give you a sign; Behold, a virgin shall conceive, and bear a son, and shall call his name Immanuel.

ISAIAH 7:14

Long before anyone had ever heard about Jesus, God made a promise. "I will send someone to save the world," He said. The world needed saving because its people did things that made God unhappy. But those people belonged to God! They were His children. He did not want to punish them for the bad things they did. So God made a plan to send His Son, Jesus, to save the world.

God's plan was perfect. He planned to send Jesus into the world as a baby. And when Jesus grew up, He would teach the people how God wanted them to live. Jesus would love the people so much that He would take all the punishment that they deserved—*forever*!

God's promise came with an extra-special surprise. Everyone who believed in Jesus would get to live in heaven one day with Jesus and God. And the best part is that God's promise was not just for those people long ago. His promise is for you!

Dear Father, it makes me happy
that You love me. Thank You
for always keeping Your
promises. Help me to keep my
promises, too.

Here We Come A-Caroling

Here we come a-caroling
Among the leaves so green,
Here we come a-wand'ring,
So fair to be seen.

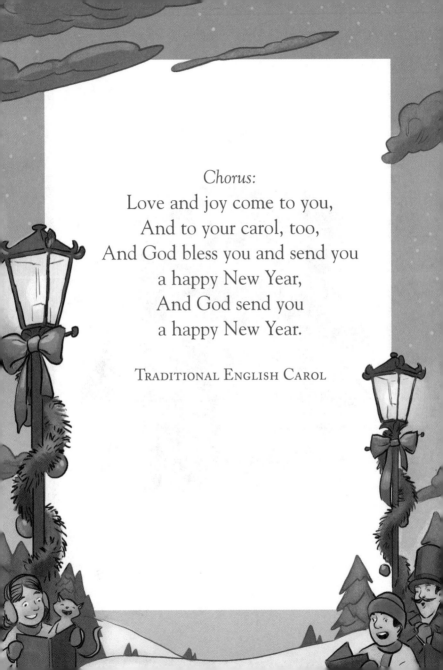

Chorus:
Love and joy come to you,
And to your carol, too,
And God bless you and send you
a happy New Year,
And God send you
a happy New Year.

TRADITIONAL ENGLISH CAROL

Patience

Wait on the LORD: be of good courage,
and he shall strengthen thine heart:
wait, I say, on the LORD.

PSALM 27:14

Has anyone ever told you to be patient?
Has anyone ever told you to wait?

Patience is what God expected from His
people. He expected them to wait for what He
had promised them. The people wanted Jesus to
come right away to save the world. But God decided they should wait.

Waiting was hard. It was like knowing they
were getting a really special present for Christmas and they had to wait until Christmas morning to open it. But while the people waited, God
gave them little hints. He told them a tiny bit
about Jesus' mother. He told them Jesus' name
and even some of His nicknames, like Immanuel

and Prince of Peace. He said that Baby Jesus would be born in a little town called Bethlehem. But God did not say *when* Jesus would come. He decided, "You will just have to wait."

So the people waited. . .and they waited. . . and they waited. They waited for days and months, and then they waited for years! As best they could, God's people waited patiently.

Dear Father, waiting is hard for me sometimes. I try my best to be patient, but it doesn't always work. So please give me the patience I need!

LITTLE CHILDREN, WAKE AND LISTEN

Little children, wake and listen!
Songs are breaking o'er the earth;
While the stars in heaven glisten,
Hear the news of Jesus' birth.

Long ago, to lovely meadows,
Angels brought the message down;
Still, each year, through
midnight shadows,
It is heard in every town.

ANONYMOUS

Trust

Some trust in chariots, and some in horses: but we will remember the name of the LORD our God.

PSALM 20:7

While they waited, God expected His people to trust Him to do exactly what He had promised. Trust means believing in someone or something with all of your heart. God wanted His people to believe with all of their hearts that He would send Jesus to save the world. But some people found it hard to trust God because they could not see Him. They trusted only in things that they *could* see, like chariots (chariots were carts that soldiers rode in) and the horses that pulled them. This made God sad.

A good plan takes time. Those who trusted God believed that His plan was good, and they understood they had to wait while God put His plan together. They believed in God's goodness, and they knew that God loved them. With all of their hearts, they believed that God's plan would work out perfectly. So those people trusted God, and they looked forward to Jesus coming to save the world.

You should trust God, too. Do you know why? Because God has a plan for you, and His plan is very good.

Dear Father, thank You for
having a good plan for me.
I believe that You love me,
and I trust You to
take care of me.

The Truth Sent from Above

This is the truth
sent from above,
The truth of God,
the God of love;
Therefore don't turn
me from your door,
But hearken all,
both rich and poor.

And at this season of the year
Our blest Redeemer did appear
He here did live,
and here did preach,
And many thousands
He did teach.

TRADITIONAL ENGLISH FOLK CAROL

A Perfect Plan

For I know the thoughts that I think toward you, saith the LORD, thoughts of peace, and not of evil,
to give you an expected end.

JEREMIAH 29:11

What seemed like a long time to God's people was just like a blink of an eye to God. His time, heaven time, is not like time here on earth. God knew exactly how He would work out His plan to send Jesus to save the world. And God knew all about Jesus long before He arrived here as a baby. After all, Jesus had been God's Son forever. He will always be God's Son.

Do you know that you are a child of God, too? You are! God made you. God knows everything about you. He knew you before you were born. He had a perfect plan to send you into the world, and He has your whole life planned out. Much of it is a secret. You will find out more about God's plan as you grow up. But His plan for you is like His plan for Jesus—perfect in every way. Part of God's plan is this: He will be your heavenly Father forever.

Dear Father, thank You for
making me and for knowing
all about me. I can't wait
to see the wonderful plan You
have for my life!

O COME, LITTLE CHILDREN

O come, little children,
from near and afar,
And gaze on the wonder
'neath Bethlehem's star.
God sent His own Son
as a dear little boy
To be your redeemer,
your hope, and your joy.

Come, kneel and adore Him
like shepherds today,
Lift up little hands now
and praise Him as they.
Rejoice that the Savior
was sent you this night,
And join in the song
of the angels of light.

CHRISTOPH VON SCHMID

Forgotten?

But the very hairs of your
head are all numbered.

MATTHEW 10:30

Some people wondered if God had forgotten about them because God had promised them Jesus but Jesus hadn't shown up yet. The people did not have to worry. God had not forgotten them. One of the amazing things about God is that He knows everything about everybody all the time, and that kind of knowing helps God make choices that are perfectly right.

God chose Jesus' mother, Mary, from among all the women in the world. And He chose Joseph to be Jesus' daddy on earth from all the world's men. Of all the places in the world, God chose the little town of Bethlehem as the place where Jesus would be born. He chose the exact day of Jesus' birth and the exact time. God's plan was coming together in a perfect way.

Do you believe that God knows everything about you? He chose your mom and dad and where and when you would be born. He chose the colors of your skin, eyes, and hair. God even chose how many hairs would be on your head! Can you count them all? God can. He knows exactly how many there are.

Dear Father, thank You for
always choosing what is best
for me. Thank You for
remembering me and knowing
everything about me.

GOD GIVE YE
MERRY CHRISTMAS TIDE

God give ye merry Christmas tide,
Ye gentle people all!
And in your merry making may
No evil chance befall:
Rejoice! for once at Bethlehem,
While shepherds knelt to pray,

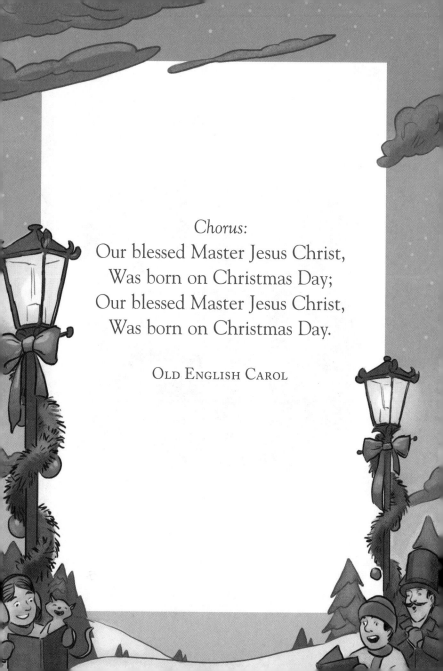

Chorus:
Our blessed Master Jesus Christ,
Was born on Christmas Day;
Our blessed Master Jesus Christ,
Was born on Christmas Day.

OLD ENGLISH CAROL

Rules

And it came to pass in those days, that there went out a decree from Caesar Augustus, that all the world should be taxed.

LUKE 2:1

Finally, God's plan was ready. It was time to send Jesus to earth. While most of God's people were waiting and wondering, God was busy. He had chosen Mary and Joseph as Jesus' earthly parents. He had planned where and when Jesus would be born. Now, God had one more thing to do. He had to get Mary and Joseph to the little town of Bethlehem. They did not live there. They lived in a place called Nazareth about eighty miles away.

So God whispered to the emperor's heart (the emperor was a leader, like a king), "Everyone must go to the city where they were born so all the people can be counted and pay their taxes." And that is exactly what the emperor did. He made a rule, and Mary and Joseph had to follow it. They had to go to Bethlehem.

When God makes rules, He expects His children to obey them. Are you a good rule follower? Can you name some important rules?

Dear Father, I know that
rules are important. Rules keep
me safe, and they help me
to learn. Help me, please,
to follow the rules.

39

O LITTLE TOWN OF BETHLEHEM

O little town of Bethlehem,
How still we see thee lie;
Above thy deep and dreamless sleep
The silent stars go by:

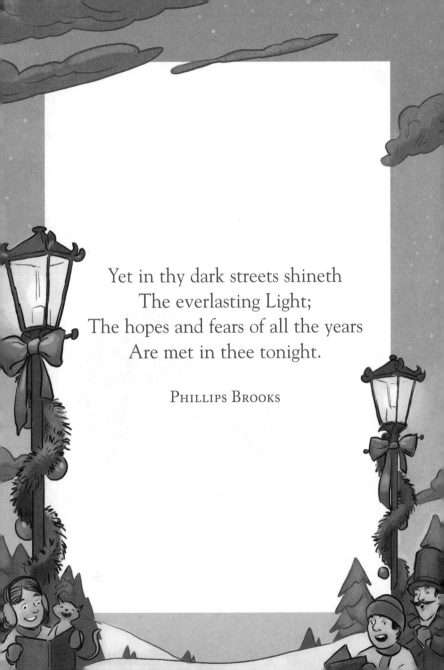

Yet in thy dark streets shineth
The everlasting Light;
The hopes and fears of all the years
Are met in thee tonight.

PHILLIPS BROOKS

Travelers

And Joseph also went up from Galilee, out of the city of Nazareth, into Judaea, unto the city of David, which is called Bethlehem; (because he was of the house and lineage of David:) to be taxed with Mary his espoused wife, being great with child.

LUKE 2:4–5

Mary and Joseph lived in a time when there were no cars, trains, or airplanes. They walked all the way to Bethlehem. Walking was hard for Mary because Baby Jesus was about to be born. Do you wonder if she and Joseph worried? What if Mary had the baby somewhere between home and Bethlehem? What if there was no one to help when the baby came?

But Mary and Joseph did not have to worry. God's angels had visited both of them, and those angels told them about their special baby. Mary and Joseph did not have to worry because God was with them all the way to Bethlehem. He protected them and little Baby Jesus, who had not yet been born.

God also goes with you wherever *you* go. You can't see Him, but He is always there. God stays with you all the time, keeping you safe and sound.

Dear Father, thank You for
staying with me. I like knowing
that wherever I go You are with
me. I like that You always keep
me safe and sound.

O Come, All Ye Faithful

O come, all ye faithful,
joyful and triumphant!
O come ye, O come ye to Bethlehem;
Come and behold him
Born the King of angels:
O come, let us adore Him,
O come, let us adore Him,
O come, let us adore Him,
Christ the Lord.

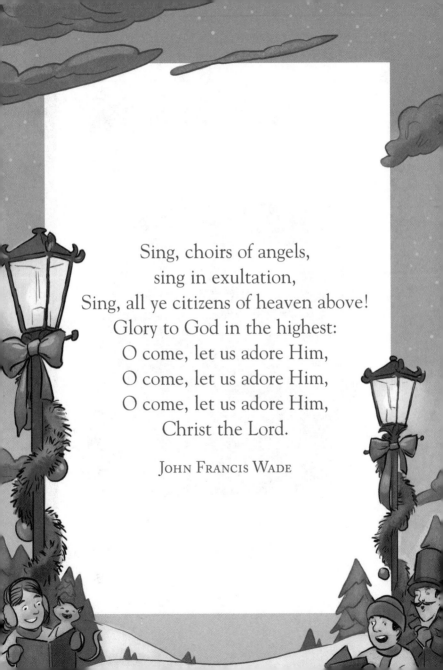

Sing, choirs of angels,
sing in exultation,
Sing, all ye citizens of heaven above!
Glory to God in the highest:
O come, let us adore Him,
O come, let us adore Him,
O come, let us adore Him,
Christ the Lord.

JOHN FRANCIS WADE

A Place to Stay

Blessed be the LORD: for he hath
shewed me his marvellous kindness
in a strong city.

PSALM 31:21

When Mary and Joseph arrived, they
must have seen that Bethlehem was filled with
people. In just a few days, the Little Town of
Bethlehem had become the Busy Town of Bethlehem. Like Joseph, everyone had returned to his
hometown to be counted and pay taxes.

When Mary and Joseph looked for a place to
stay, all the rooms were taken. But they did not
have to worry, because God had a plan.

A kind innkeeper knew where they could
stay. Some people believe they stayed in a stable.
Others think it was a cave. But where Mary and
Joseph stayed is not as important as God's plan
for them. He already knew where Jesus would be

born—in a simple place among the animals. And when Baby Jesus came, Mary wrapped Him up, all toasty warm, and laid Him in a manger. (A manger is a long, open box for farm animals to eat from.)

Kind people, like the innkeeper in the story, are God's special helpers. How was the innkeeper kind? How can you be kind to others?

Dear Father, You are always so kind to me! Let me be Your special helper. Teach me to be kind to others.

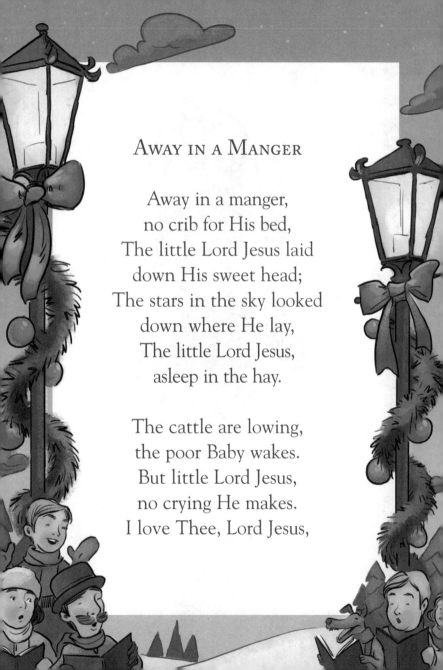

AWAY IN A MANGER

Away in a manger,
no crib for His bed,
The little Lord Jesus laid
down His sweet head;
The stars in the sky looked
down where He lay,
The little Lord Jesus,
asleep in the hay.

The cattle are lowing,
the poor Baby wakes.
But little Lord Jesus,
no crying He makes.
I love Thee, Lord Jesus,

look down from the sky.
And stay by the cradle
till morning is nigh.

Be near me, Lord Jesus,
I ask Thee to stay
Close by me forever,
and love me, I pray!
Bless all the dear children
in Thy tender care
And take us to heaven,
to live with Thee there.

Unknown

Silent Night

Be silent, O all flesh, before the LORD:
for he is raised up out of
his holy habitation.

ZECHARIAH 2:13

Mary and Joseph knew that Baby Jesus was the One God had promised to send, but no one else in Bethlehem knew. At that very minute when Jesus was born, no one was waiting for Him to come. Most people were sound asleep in their beds not knowing that something wonderful had just happened. The night was starry and silent except for the sound of a baby crying.

But God was there. He was there on that silent night watching over Baby Jesus, Mary, Joseph, and all the people in the world. God's plan was unfolding, and He was about to do something big. God was about to send some special messengers down to earth.

Do you know that God is with you all through the night? He is! Just as He was with Baby Jesus on that night long ago, God is with you, too. God never sleeps. When you are sound asleep in your bed and the night is dark and your house is silent, God is right there watching over you. Isn't that wonderful?

Dear Father, bless me as I sleep
tonight. Be with my family
and me. And please give us
a good night's sleep and many
happy dreams.

SILENT NIGHT

Silent night! Holy night!
All is calm, all is bright,
Round yon Virgin Mother and Child!
Holy Infant, so tender and mild,
Sleep in heavenly peace!
Sleep in heavenly peace!

Silent night! Holy night!
Sleeps the world in peace tonight.
God sends His Son to earth below,
A Child from whom all blessings flow.
Jesus embraces mankind.
Jesus embraces mankind.

JOSEPH MOHR

Shepherds

And there were in the same country shepherds abiding in the field, keeping watch over their flock by night. And, lo, the angel of the Lord came upon them, and the glory of the Lord shone round about them: and they were sore afraid.

LUKE 2:8–9

Near Bethlehem that night, in the fields, shepherds watched their flocks of sheep. A shepherd's job is to care for his sheep, so God knew the shepherds would be awake. He sent them an angel. The angel came in a very bright light. At first the shepherds were afraid, but the angel told them, "Do not be afraid! I have come to give you Good News. A baby was born tonight in Bethlehem. He is the One God promised would come to save the world." The angel told the shepherds where to find Jesus, and then—the sky filled up with angels praising God!

God surprised the shepherds with Good News brought by angels. God likes surprising His people with wonderful things. These gifts from God are called blessings. Jesus is the best blessing of all because He came to show us the way to heaven. What other blessings can you think of?

Dear Father, thank You for sending us Jesus. He is the best blessing of all. And thank You for my family, my home, and all of Your blessings!

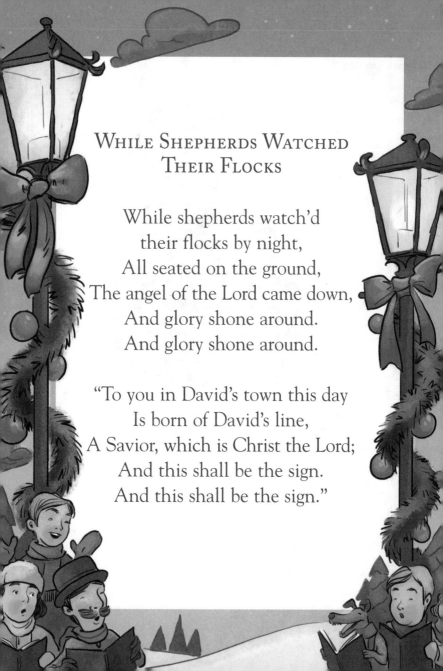

While Shepherds Watched Their Flocks

While shepherds watch'd
their flocks by night,
All seated on the ground,
The angel of the Lord came down,
And glory shone around.
And glory shone around.

"To you in David's town this day
Is born of David's line,
A Savior, which is Christ the Lord;
And this shall be the sign.
And this shall be the sign."

"The heav'nly Babe
you there shall find
To human view display'd.
All meanly wrapped
in swaddling bands,
And in a manger laid.
And in a manger laid."

NAHUM TATE

The Star

When they saw the star, they rejoiced
with exceeding great joy.

MATTHEW 2:10

On that silent, dark night when Jesus was born, God brought light into the world. The angels came to the shepherds in a big burst of light. But that was not all God did. He put a bright star up in the sky right above Jesus. That bright star, Jesus' star, could be seen from far away. God did not want to keep the Good News about Jesus a secret. He wanted people near and far to know that Jesus had come to the world. The big, bright star would lead them to where Jesus was.

God is in charge of everything. He made the sky and everything in it. So when God wanted a new star to appear, He made it happen. Do you know that God named all the stars? He knows each one. And, even better, He made you and

He knows you. God knows everyone—all the people who have ever lived on earth, all the people who live here now, and all the people who will live here in the future. That is how great and wonderful God is!

Dear Father, I think it is special that You made the sky and know all the stars. And I think it is really special that You made and know me.

STAR OF BETHLEHEM, SWEETLY SHINING

Star of Bethlehem, sweetly shining,
Let thy peaceful light
Lead us where the Christ is lying,

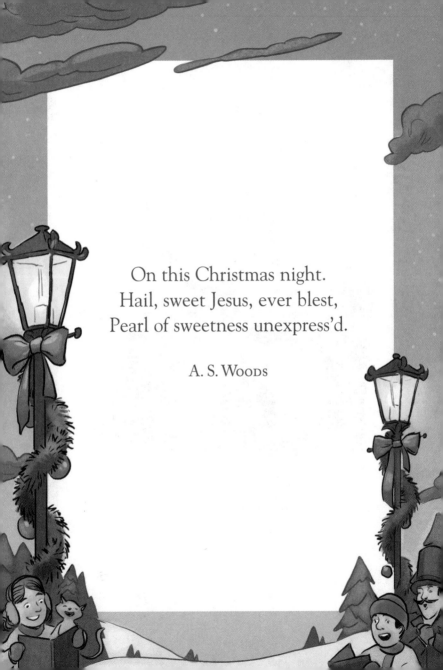

On this Christmas night.
Hail, sweet Jesus, ever blest,
Pearl of sweetness unexpress'd.

A. S. WOODS

Angels

For he shall give his angels charge over thee, to keep thee in all thy ways.

Angels are God's special messengers. Almost a year before Jesus was born, God sent an angel to Mary. This angel, named Gabriel, surprised Mary. He told her that God had chosen her to be Jesus' mother. Can you imagine how Mary must have felt? Gabriel told her that the baby's name should be "Jesus." Then God sent another angel to Joseph in a dream. That angel told Joseph to be a good husband to Mary.

Angels played a big part in the Christmas story—the story of Jesus' birthday. They were there the night Jesus was born. They shared the Good News with the shepherds, and they sang songs of joy.

Today God still sends angels to earth to do

His work. Angels are all around, but you cannot see them. God promised to send His angels to watch over His people, and God always keeps His promises. Right now, His angels are busy working. Do you know what they are doing? They are watching over you!

Dear Father, I feel good
knowing that Your angels are all
around me all the time.
Thank You for sending them
to watch over me.

ANGELS WE HAVE HEARD ON HIGH

Angels we have heard on high
Sweetly singing o'er the plains,
And the mountains in reply
Echoing their joyous strains.

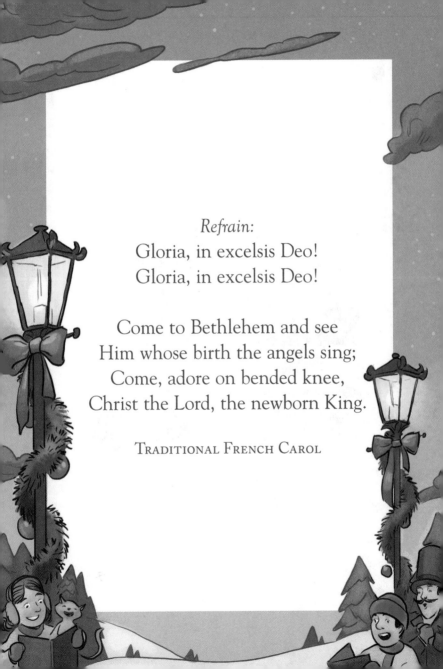

Refrain:
Gloria, in excelsis Deo!
Gloria, in excelsis Deo!

Come to Bethlehem and see
Him whose birth the angels sing;
Come, adore on bended knee,
Christ the Lord, the newborn King.

TRADITIONAL FRENCH CAROL

Baby Jesus

For unto us a child is born, unto us a son is given: and the government shall be upon his shoulder: and his name shall be called Wonderful, Counsellor, The mighty God, The everlasting Father, The Prince of Peace.

ISAIAH 9:6

IF you had seen Baby Jesus on the night He was born, you would have thought He looked like any other baby. But Jesus was a very special baby. There never had been and there never will be another baby like Him.

Baby Jesus was God's own Son. He was God Himself come down to the earth in a human body. Baby Jesus was perfect in every way. And when He grew up, Jesus would keep on being perfect. He would say and do things to amaze people, things that only God can do.

Jesus is the world's great heavenly King, and today He sits in heaven on a throne right next to God's. Someday when you get to heaven, you will see Jesus all grown up. And He will be happy to see you. One of the many wonderful things about Jesus is that He is with you all the time, now and forever. Why? Because Jesus loves you!

Dear Jesus, I feel happy that
You came down to earth, and I
am happy that I will see You one
day. Thank You for loving me.
I love You, too!

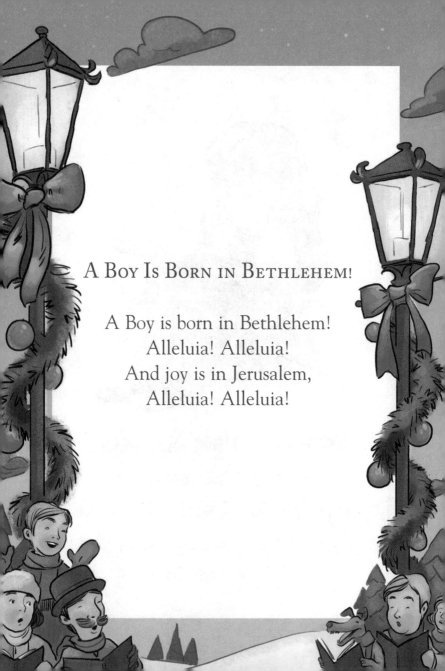

A Boy Is Born in Bethlehem!

A Boy is born in Bethlehem!
Alleluia! Alleluia!
And joy is in Jerusalem,
Alleluia! Alleluia!

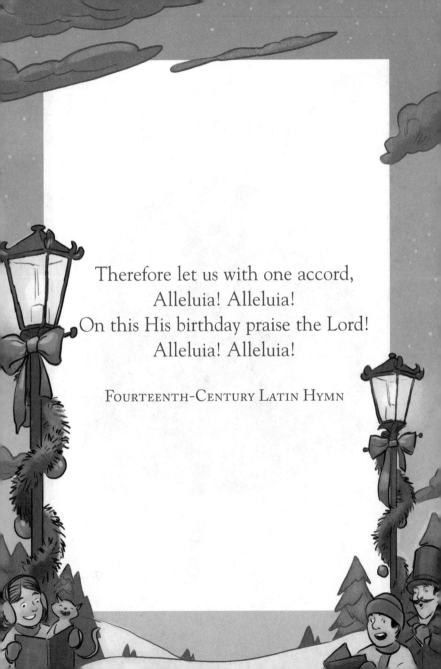

Therefore let us with one accord,
Alleluia! Alleluia!
On this His birthday praise the Lord!
Alleluia! Alleluia!

FOURTEENTH-CENTURY LATIN HYMN

Praise God!

And the shepherds returned,
glorifying and praising God for all the
things that they had heard and seen,
as it was told unto them.

LUKE 2:20

When the angels appeared to shepherds in the fields, they praised God. Do you know what "praise" means? Praise is when you say something to God that shows you respect, appreciate, and love Him. "I love You, God!" "You are so great." "Thank You for blessing me." Those are a few things that you could say to praise God.

After the angels told the shepherds about Jesus, the shepherds hurried to find the baby boy. When they found Him, they praised Him. The shepherds knew that Baby Jesus was a special gift from God. And when they went back to the fields with their sheep, the shepherds praised God all the way. They thanked Him for what the angels told them. They thanked Him for Jesus and for all the wonderful things they saw that night.

You should praise God, too. God loves it when His children praise Him. Praise Him because He loves You. Praise Him for all the wonderful things He does. Praise Him just because He is God.

Dear God, You are so wonderful!
Thank You for all the ways that
You bless me. I praise You for
being the one and only God.

PRAISE GOD THE LORD, YE SONS OF MEN

Praise God the Lord, ye sons of men,
Before His highest throne;
Today He opens heaven again
And gives us His own Son.
And gives us His own Son.

He leaves His heavenly
Father's throne,
Is born an infant small,
And in a manger, poor and lone,
Lies in a humble stall.
Lies in a humble stall.

W. Nikolaus Herman

The Wise Men

Now when Jesus was born in Bethlehem
of Judaea in the days of Herod the king,
behold, there came wise men from the east
to Jerusalem, saying, Where is he
that is born King of the Jews? for we
have seen his star in the east,
and are come to worship him.

MATTHEW 2:1–2

After Jesus was born, men traveled a long way to see Him. These men were powerful leaders who enjoyed studying the stars. When they saw Jesus' star, they wanted to follow it so they could find Him. They wanted to praise and worship Jesus and bring Him gifts. These men were very wise. Along with many other things, they knew that the stars in the sky would help them find their way. They knew that certain stars pointed north, south, east, and west. And they knew that following the biggest, brightest star would lead them to Jesus.

Being wise means being smart. Wisdom comes from God. You become wise by learning, and if you ask God He will help you to learn. Learning about God is important. Learning His ways will make you wise like the wise men. Then you can share your wisdom with others.

Dear Father, I want to be wise, so help me to learn. I know that learning is important. Teach me Your ways so I can share them with my family and friends.

WE THREE KINGS OF ORIENT ARE

We three kings of Orient are
Bearing gifts we traverse afar.
Field and fountain,
moor and mountain,
Following yonder star.

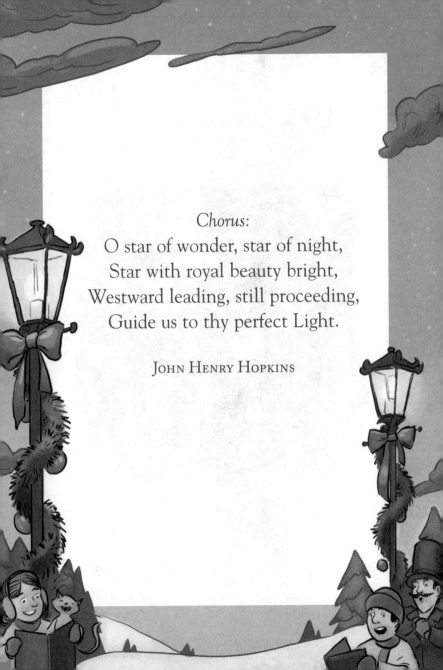

Chorus:
O star of wonder, star of night,
Star with royal beauty bright,
Westward leading, still proceeding,
Guide us to thy perfect Light.

JOHN HENRY HOPKINS

Which Way?

Ask, and it shall be given you; seek, and ye shall find; knock, and it shall be opened unto you: for every one that asketh receiveth; and he that seeketh findeth; and to him that knocketh it shall be opened.

MATTHEW 7:7–8

As smart as the wise men were, they still stopped and asked for directions. In a city called Jerusalem they asked its king, a man named Herod, for help. They said, "Where is he that is born King of the Jews? for we have seen his star in the east, and are come to worship him" (Matthew 2:2).

The king did not know where Jesus was, so he called his men together and asked if they knew. Some had heard of God's promise to send someone to save the world. Others knew that Jesus would be born in Bethlehem. So King Herod told the wise men to go to Bethlehem to search for Jesus.

Whenever you need directions, you can ask someone to help you. You can ask God. He knows everything. When you pray and ask God what to do, He promises to show you the way—and His way is always right.

Dear Father, sometimes I can't
make up my mind about
what to do. Remind me that
I can always ask You, and You
will show me the way.

WHEN CHRIST WAS BORN
IN BETHLEHEM

When Christ was born in Bethlehem,
'Twas night, but seemed
the noon of day;
The stars, whose light

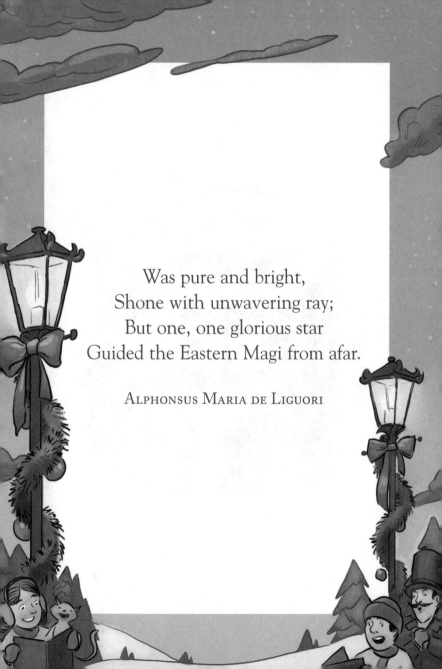

Was pure and bright,
Shone with unwavering ray;
But one, one glorious star
Guided the Eastern Magi from afar.

ALPHONSUS MARIA DE LIGUORI

King Herod

Behold, the angel of the Lord appeareth to Joseph in a dream, saying, Arise, and take the young child and his mother, and flee into Egypt, and be thou there until I bring thee word: for Herod will seek the young child to destroy him.

MATTHEW 2:13

Another name for Jesus is King of the Jews. There will never be another king as great as He. But not every king is good. King Herod was a bad king. He wanted all the power, and he was jealous of Baby Jesus. He did not like it that God wanted Jesus to grow up and lead the people.

So Herod made an awful plan. He planned to kill Baby Jesus. But God was not going to let that happen! He sent an angel to warn Joseph. Then Joseph took Mary and Jesus to a place called Egypt, and they stayed there until it was safe to go home.

God wants the world ruled by good leaders. Someday when you are old enough, you can help decide who your leaders should be. But for now, you can do this: you can pray for leaders everywhere.

Dear Father, I pray that all the world's leaders will love You and follow Your rules. And thank You, God, for making Jesus the one great King.

THE CHILDREN'S KING

No courtiers greet His birth await,
Though He is King of glory,
But through the sky the angels fly
To tell the wondrous story.

Chorus:
The children's King,
the children's King,
O come let us adore Him;
Our carols bring, His praises sing,
All kneeling low before Him.

When told His name,
the shepherds came
Where that dear Babe was sleeping;
We haste with them to Bethlehem,
Our happy Christmas keeping.

UNKNOWN

Finding Jesus

But sanctify the Lord God in your hearts: and be ready always to give an answer to every man that asketh you a reason of the hope that is in you with meekness and fear.

1 PETER 3:15

There were no cars, buses, trains, or airplanes in Jesus' time. The wise men walked and rode on camels while they followed the star to Bethlehem. They traveled a long way, in all kinds of weather, through deserts and over hills. Some people think it took the wise men months or even years to find the place where the star shone brightly overhead.

Finding Jesus meant so much to the wise men that they were willing to travel a long way and a long time to get to Him. They knew that Jesus was God's great King, and finding Him was something very special.

Do you know that you can find Jesus, too? You can! And you do not have to travel to find Him. Jesus lives in heaven with God, but He can also live inside your heart—in the place that love comes from. Jesus loves you so much that He will be with you forever.

Dear Jesus, thank You for living
inside my heart and loving me
all the time. I am glad that You
were born and that God sent
You to love me.

Jesus Loves Me

Jesus loves me! This I know,
For the Bible tells me so;
Little ones to Him belong;
They are weak, but He is strong.

Refrain:
Yes, Jesus loves me!
Yes, Jesus loves me!
Yes, Jesus loves me!
The Bible tells me so.

Anna B. Warner

Treasures

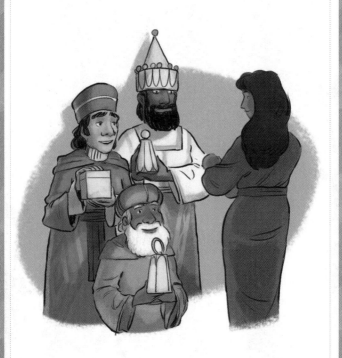

And when they were come into the
house, they saw the young child with
Mary his mother, and fell down,
and worshipped him: and when they
had opened their treasures,
they presented unto him gifts; gold,
and frankincense and myrrh.

MATTHEW 2:11

When the wise men arrived in Bethlehem, Jesus' star hung in the sky right above the place where He lived. They had found Him!

The wise men had carried precious gifts for Him all the way from the East, treasures called gold, frankincense, and myrrh. These were presents fit for a king. Gold was like money, and frankincense and myrrh were special spices that smelled wonderful. The wise men brought Jesus their most valuable gifts because they knew who He was—God's Son, the great King who would grow up to save the world. The men gave Jesus His gifts, and they knelt down and worshipped Him because they were worshipping God.

If you could give a special gift to Jesus, what would it be? He doesn't expect you to give Him gold, or sweet-smelling spices. Your gift does not have to cost any money. The very best gift you can give Jesus is your love. Love is the greatest gift of all.

Dear Jesus, I have a very special
gift for You. This is what it is:
I will give You my love today,
tomorrow, and forever!

Oh, How I Love Jesus

There is a Name I love to hear,
I love to sing its worth;
It sounds like music in my ear,
The sweetest Name on earth.

Refrain:
Oh, how I love Jesus,
Oh, how I love Jesus,
Oh, how I love Jesus,
Because He first loved me!

FREDERICK WHITFIELD

Wonderful Jesus!

For God so loved the world, that he gave
his only begotten Son, that whosoever
believeth in him should not perish,
but have everlasting life.

JOHN 3:16

There are so many wonderful things about Jesus that make Him special. The most important is that Jesus is still here today. You cannot see Him, but He is just as real now as He was on that first Christmas when God sent Him to earth as a baby. Jesus was sent here to love and help people forever.

Jesus is God's Son. He is part of God, and He can do all of the wonderful things that God can do. Best of all, if you believe Jesus came to the world to save people from their sins, Jesus will help you get to heaven someday. And when you get there, you will be with Jesus and God and all the other people who have believed in Him. Heaven is a wonderful, happy place where people live forever. They never die!

Jesus loves children like you. He watches over you every minute of each day, and you can talk to Him whenever you want to just by praying.

What is your favorite thing about Jesus?

Dear Jesus, I like hearing the
true story about You when You
were a baby. And I love knowing
that You are all grown up now
and watching over me.

JOY TO THE WORLD!

Joy to the world! The Lord is come.
Let earth receive her King;
Let every heart prepare Him room;
And heav'n and nature sing,
And heav'n and nature sing,
And heav'n and heav'n
and nature sing.

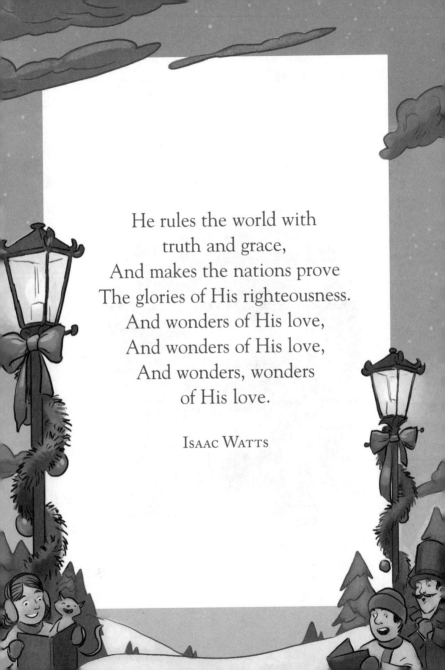

He rules the world with
truth and grace,
And makes the nations prove
The glories of His righteousness.
And wonders of His love,
And wonders of His love,
And wonders, wonders
of His love.

ISAAC WATTS

What Is Christmas?

And the child grew, and waxed strong in spirit, filled with wisdom: and the grace of God was upon him.

LUKE 2:40

Christmas Day, December 25, is when the whole world celebrates Jesus' birthday. The celebration is not just one day long. People spend several weeks getting ready and celebrating with their family and friends. They read the Bible story that tells about Jesus' birth, and they go to church to learn more about Christmas. People decorate for Jesus' birthday, and they sing Christmas carols about Him.

Christmas reminds us of Baby Jesus in the manger, angels, shepherds, the star, and the wise men. It is a time to share gifts and treats and to enjoy little surprises. The closer it gets to Christmas, the more excited people become. They have waited all year for Christmas, as the people of long ago waited for Jesus to be born.

God wants people to always remember that Christmas is about Jesus' birthday. It is a time to celebrate Jesus' coming into the world, and it is a time to thank God for giving us Jesus—His most wonderful gift.

Dear Father, thank You for
teaching me that Jesus is the
only reason that we celebrate
Christmas. On Christmas Day
I will remember to say,
"Happy birthday, Jesus!"

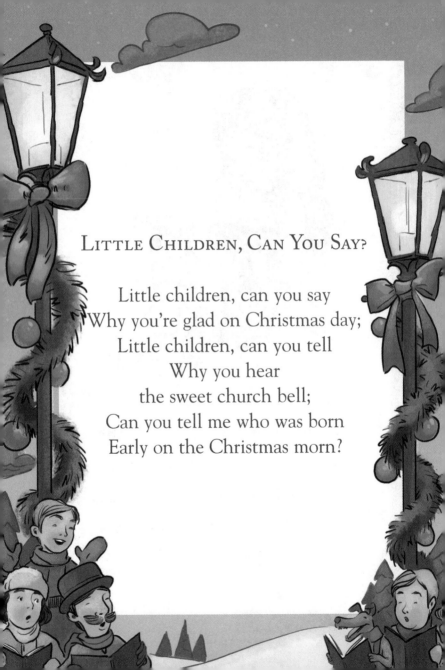

LITTLE CHILDREN, CAN YOU SAY?

Little children, can you say
Why you're glad on Christmas day;
Little children, can you tell
Why you hear
the sweet church bell;
Can you tell me who was born
Early on the Christmas morn?

This is the birthday of our King,
And we our little offering bring—
This is our Savior's holiday,
And therefore we are glad today;
We'll sing and pray
and read His Word,
And keep the birthday
of our Lord.

UNKNOWN

Good News!

And he said unto them,
Go ye into all the world, and preach
the gospel to every creature.

MARK 16:15

Sometimes the story of Jesus is called the Good News. On that very first Christmas, God sent His own Son, Jesus, into the world to save people and make a way for them to get to heaven. God wants everyone to spread that Good News so the whole world will know.

The shepherds were the first to share it. After they saw Baby Jesus, they told everyone they met. They told about the angel coming to them in the fields saying, "Do not be afraid! I have come to give you Good News. A baby was born tonight in Bethlehem. He is the One God promised would come to save the world." And those people the shepherds told shared the Good News with others, and the Good News kept going. . .and going. . .and going. . .and it is still being shared today.

You can help tell the world about Jesus. Tell your friends and family. Ask them to share the Good News, too: Jesus came to save the world and to show God's people the way to heaven!

Dear Father, teach me more
about Jesus so I can tell all
about Him. I want to share the
Good News with everyone.

GO, TELL IT ON THE MOUNTAIN

Refrain:
Go, tell it on the mountain,
Over the hills and everywhere.
Go, tell it on the mountain,
That Jesus Christ is born.

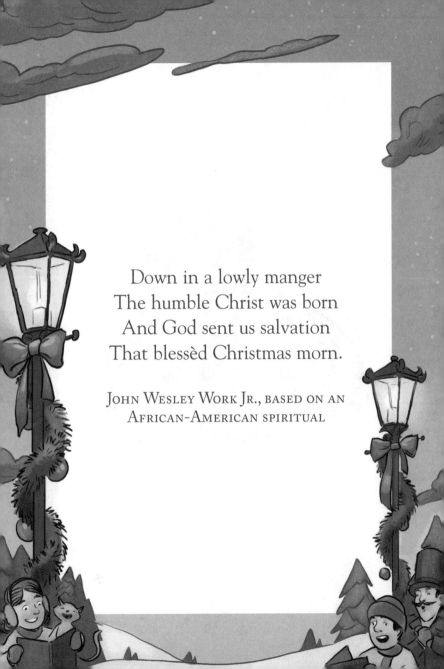

Down in a lowly manger
The humble Christ was born
And God sent us salvation
That blessèd Christmas morn.

JOHN WESLEY WORK JR., BASED ON AN
AFRICAN-AMERICAN SPIRITUAL

Peace on Earth

The wolf also shall dwell with the lamb, and the leopard shall lie down with the kid; and the calf and the young lion and the fatling together; and a little child shall lead them.

ISAIAH 11:6

Christmas is a happy time, and it is a peaceful time. Peaceful means "quiet" and "gentle." God wants everyone to be at peace with one another. He wants everyone to get along. One reason God sent Jesus to earth was to bring peace to the world. Someday, all people on earth will live peacefully together, and that will be because of Jesus. Even animals that do not get along will live together peacefully.

Animals were there the night Jesus was born. Animals might have been the first to see Baby Jesus. Some people think that Mary rode to

Bethlehem on a donkey. So a donkey might have been there. And Jesus was born in a place where animals stayed. His bed was their feeding box. Maybe cows and goats were there. The shepherds might have brought their sheep. Do you think the animals got along peacefully with one another?

How can you bring peace to your house?

Dear Father, please help me to get along with my family and friends. I think it feels good to be peaceful. I want everybody on earth to get along.

THE FRIENDLY BEASTS

Jesus our brother, kind and good
Was humbly born in a stable rude
And the friendly beasts
around Him stood,
Jesus our brother, kind and good.

"I," said the donkey, shaggy and brown,
"I carried His mother up hill and down;
I carried her safely
to Bethlehem town.
"I," said the donkey,
shaggy and brown.

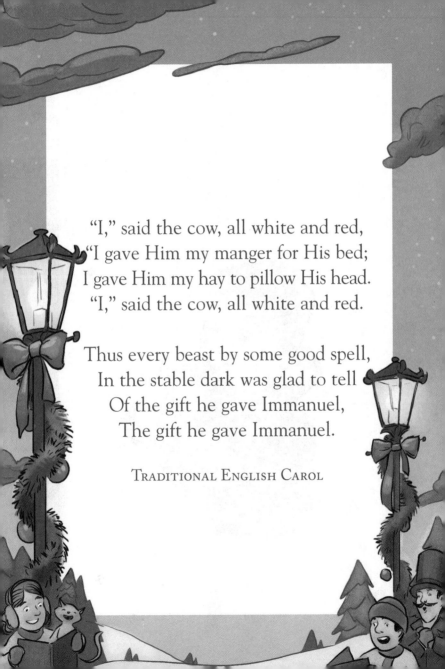

"I," said the cow, all white and red,
"I gave Him my manger for His bed;
I gave Him my hay to pillow His head.
"I," said the cow, all white and red.

Thus every beast by some good spell,
In the stable dark was glad to tell
Of the gift he gave Immanuel,
The gift he gave Immanuel.

TRADITIONAL ENGLISH CAROL

Light of the World

As long as I am in the world,
I am the light of the world.

JOHN 9:5

Light was an important part of that first Christmas long ago. On the night Jesus was born, the angels came to the shepherds in a great, bright light, and Jesus' star lit up the sky to show the way to Bethlehem.

Today at Christmastime, people use light to celebrate Jesus' birthday. They decorate their houses with Christmas lights and put lights on Christmas trees. Candlelight is a part of Christmas, too. Candles light up churches, and some people light candles in their houses.

Another name for Jesus is "the Light of the World." That is because when He grew up, Jesus told people, "I am the light of the world" (John 8:12). He meant that He would help all the people in the world see the way to heaven. Jesus' love is like a bright, warm light. Believing that He came to show the way to heaven is like seeing Him shine a dazzling light on a dark path.

Whenever you see Christmas lights, think about Jesus. Remember the angels appearing to the shepherds in a burst of white light, and remember Jesus' star shining brightly in the sky.

Dear Jesus, from now on when I see Christmas lights, I will think of You and remember Your birthday. Thank You for being the Light of the World.

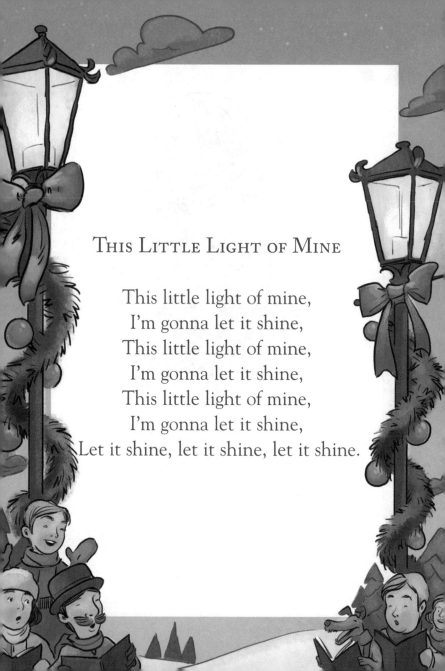

THIS LITTLE LIGHT OF MINE

This little light of mine,
I'm gonna let it shine,
This little light of mine,
I'm gonna let it shine,
This little light of mine,
I'm gonna let it shine,
Let it shine, let it shine, let it shine.

Everywhere I go,
I'm gonna let it shine,
Everywhere I go,
I'm gonna let it shine,
Everywhere I go,
I'm gonna let it shine,
Let it shine, let it shine,
let it shine.

HARRY DIXON LOES

Christmas
Dinner

But when thou makest a feast,
call the poor, the maimed, the lame,
the blind: and thou shalt be blessed;
for they cannot recompense thee:
for thou shalt be recompensed at the
resurrection of the just.

LUKE 14:13–14

In Jesus' time, people celebrated special days with a feast—a big dinner. People do the same today, especially on holidays like Christmas. People remember Jesus' birthday with Christmas dinner. Turkey, ham, potatoes, vegetables, pies, cakes: There is so much yummy food to eat and plenty left over to share.

Jesus reminded people to share their feast with others, especially those who do not have enough. One way that people share their food is by giving some to food banks. Community helpers collect food to give to the hungry. Jesus said that when people give something away, they should expect nothing in return. Giving to help someone makes you feel good. And when Jesus sees you giving, that makes Him feel good, too.

Talk with your family about giving. Why is it important to share what you have with those who do not have enough? How can you help the hungry?

Dear Father, I want everyone to
have a happy time celebrating
Jesus' birthday. Remind me to
share what I have and to give to
those who do not have enough.

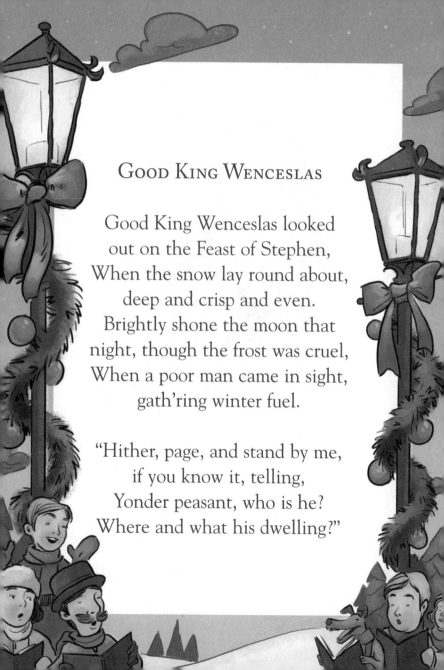

GOOD KING WENCESLAS

Good King Wenceslas looked
out on the Feast of Stephen,
When the snow lay round about,
deep and crisp and even.
Brightly shone the moon that
night, though the frost was cruel,
When a poor man came in sight,
gath'ring winter fuel.

"Hither, page, and stand by me,
if you know it, telling,
Yonder peasant, who is he?
Where and what his dwelling?"

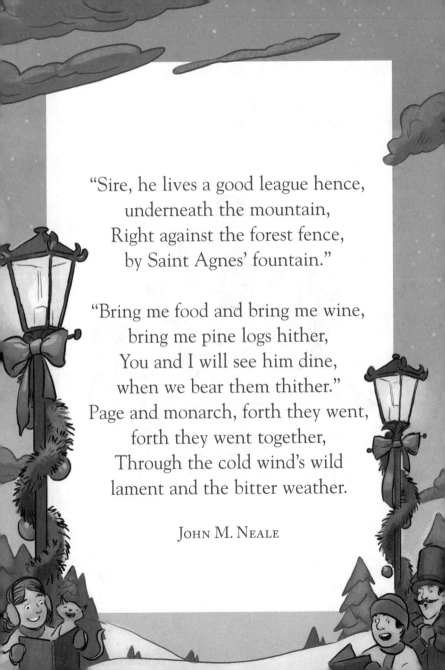

"Sire, he lives a good league hence,
underneath the mountain,
Right against the forest fence,
by Saint Agnes' fountain."

"Bring me food and bring me wine,
bring me pine logs hither,
You and I will see him dine,
when we bear them thither."
Page and monarch, forth they went,
forth they went together,
Through the cold wind's wild
lament and the bitter weather.

JOHN M. NEALE

Family Time

[I] will be a Father unto you,
and ye shall be my sons and daughters,
saith the Lord Almighty.
2 CORINTHIANS 6:18

Christmas is a special time for
families. Moms, dads, sons, daughters, sisters, brothers, aunts, uncles, cousins, grandparents—they all get together to celebrate Jesus' birthday!

Families around the world celebrate in different ways. In South Africa, Christmas comes in summertime. Instead of a big Christmas dinner, families get together for a barbeque lunch. In Mexico, people walk down the streets singing Christmas songs as they remember Mary and Joseph looking for a place to stay in Bethlehem. In Germany, children write letters to Baby Jesus and leave them on windowsills. All over the world going to church is an important part of a family Christmas.

Families wish each other "Merry Christmas" in different ways. In France they say, *"Joyeux Noel."* In Mexico: *"Feliz Navidad."* And in Hawaii: *"Mele Kalikimaka."*

Families come in many sizes. Some are big. Some are small. But all families who believe that Jesus came to save the world are part of God's one big family. He is the heavenly Father, and they are His children.

Does your family have a special way to celebrate Christmas?

Dear Father, thank You for my
family. And thank You for
being my heavenly Father.
I feel special knowing that
I belong to You.

DECK THE HALLS

Deck the halls with boughs of holly,
Fa la la la la, la la la la,
'Tis the season to be jolly,
Fa la la la la, la la la la.

Don we now our gay apparel,
Fa la la la la, la la la la,
Troll the ancient Christmas carol,
Fa la la la la, la la la la.

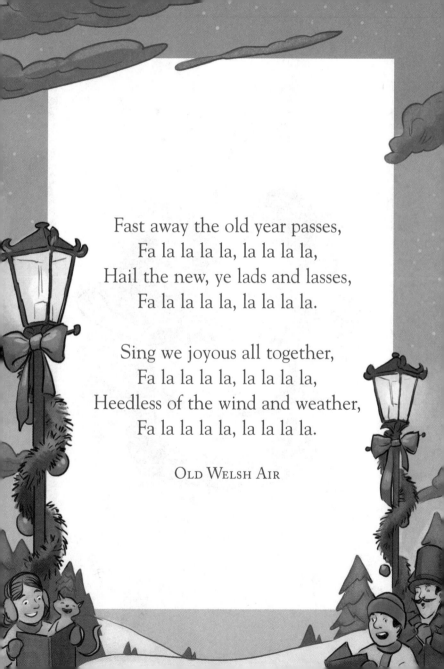

Fast away the old year passes,
Fa la la la la, la la la la,
Hail the new, ye lads and lasses,
Fa la la la la, la la la la.

Sing we joyous all together,
Fa la la la la, la la la la,
Heedless of the wind and weather,
Fa la la la la, la la la la.

OLD WELSH AIR

Friends!

> Ye are my friends, if ye do
> whatsoever I command you.
>
> JOHN 15:14

Friends have fun celebrating Christmas together. There are so many things to do. Friends bake Christmas cookies and make a birthday cake for Jesus. They sing Christmas carols and make little gifts and surprises. Friends act in Christmas plays at church, and they hear about Jesus' birthday in Sunday school. They decorate Christmas trees together and play games and wish each other a "Merry Christmas!"

Jesus loved spending time with His friends. He liked visiting two sisters and a brother named Mary, Martha, and Lazarus. And Jesus had twelve helper-friends called *disciples*. They were Peter, Andrew, James and James (two Jameses!), John, Philip, Bartholomew, Matthew, Thomas,

Simon, Thaddeus, and Judas Iscariot. Do you have any friends with those names?

Jesus made friends everywhere He went, and He is your friend, too! Jesus is your best friend because He knows you better than anyone else. He loves you just the way you are, and He always has time for you. Jesus helps you and watches over you day and night.

What do you and your friends do together to celebrate His birthday?

Dear Jesus, You are my best
friend. I like it that You love me
just as I am and that You
always have time for me. I can
tell You anything and know that
You will hear me.

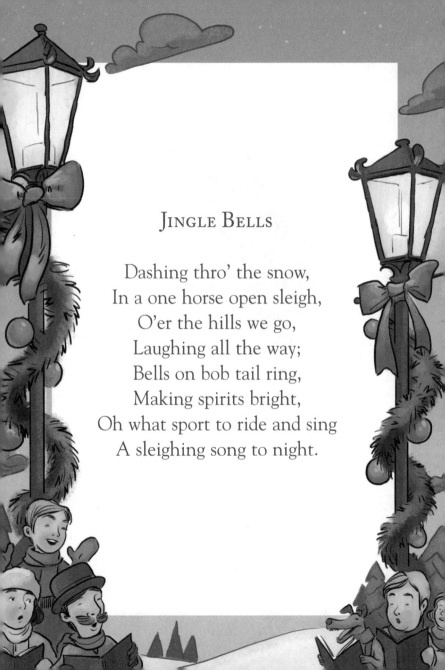

JINGLE BELLS

Dashing thro' the snow,
In a one horse open sleigh,
O'er the hills we go,
Laughing all the way;
Bells on bob tail ring,
Making spirits bright,
Oh what sport to ride and sing
A sleighing song to night.

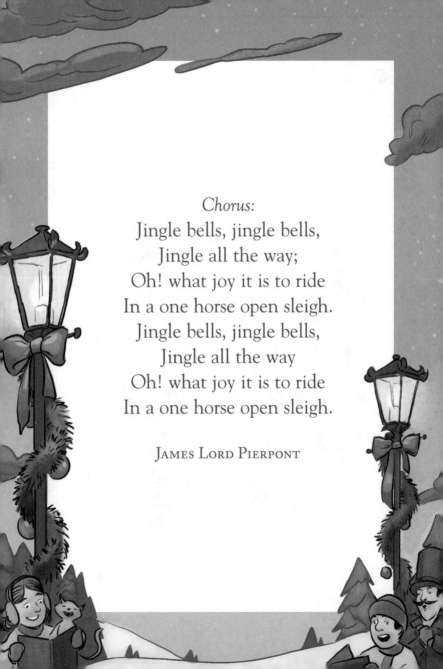

Chorus:
Jingle bells, jingle bells,
Jingle all the way;
Oh! what joy it is to ride
In a one horse open sleigh.
Jingle bells, jingle bells,
Jingle all the way
Oh! what joy it is to ride
In a one horse open sleigh.

JAMES LORD PIERPONT

Christmas
Wishes

A new commandment I give unto you,
that ye love one another; as I have loved
you, that ye also love one another.

Some people wish for big things that are new and special. Some wish for everyday things like a warm house, clean clothes, and plenty of food to eat. Some wish for friends.

All year, and especially at Christmas, you can help people get what they wish for by being God's helper.

Jesus loved everybody, and when He grew up He helped many people. When they were sick, Jesus helped them to be well again. When they were hungry, He found ways to feed them. But most of all, Jesus taught people to love and help one another.

You can help at Christmastime by thinking

about what people need and then finding ways to make their wishes come true. Maybe your Sunday school class can visit lonely people in nursing homes or help older people in your church with yard work or snow shoveling.

Talk with your family about ways that you can help others at Christmas. See if you can make someone's wishes come true.

Dear Father, I want to help
people not just at Christmas but
every day. Help me to see what
they need. Then give me ideas for
ways I can help.

WE WISH YOU A MERRY CHRISTMAS

We wish you a merry Christmas,
We wish you a merry Christmas,
We wish you a merry Christmas,
And a happy New Year!

Refrain:
Good tidings we bring
for you and your kin;
We wish you a merry Christmas
and a happy New Year!

Traditional English Carol

Christmas Eve

And one cried unto another, and said,
Holy, holy, holy, is the LORD of hosts:
the whole earth is full of his glory.

ISAIAH 6:3

Christmas Eve is a holy night.
That means it is a night to spend thinking about
God. People wait all year for Christmas Eve.
They wait like those people from long ago waited
for God to keep His promise. But people today
know that God *did* keep His promise! He sent
Jesus to save the world, and Christmas Eve is
one special night to remember and celebrate that
promise. It is a night to think about Mary and
Joseph going to Bethlehem, Jesus in the manger,
angels, shepherds, and wise men. It is a night for
church and candlelight and thanking God for
His wonderful gifts.

People celebrate Christmas with lights, trees,

cookies, songs, and presents, but Jesus is much more important than those things. He is the one true reason that Christmas is celebrated all around the world. If God had not kept His promise to send Jesus, there would be no Christmas. It would be just like any other day.

Ask someone to read aloud the Christmas story in the Bible: Luke 2:1–20.

Dear Father, I love celebrating
Jesus' birthday! Thank You
for sending Him to earth.
And thank You for teaching
me about Him and the real
meaning of Christmas.

O HOLY NIGHT

O holy night, the stars
are brightly shining,
It is the night of the
dear Savior's birth;
Long lay the world in sin
and error pining,
'Till He appeared and
the soul felt its worth.
A thrill of hope the
weary world rejoices,
For yonder breaks a new
and glorious morn.

Chorus:
Fall on your knees!
Oh, hear the angel voices!
O night divine!
O night when Christ was born.
O night, O holy night,
O night divine.

PLACIDE CAPPEAU

Presents!

Every good gift and every perfect gift
is from above, and cometh down from
the Father of lights, with whom is no
variableness, neither shadow of turning.

JAMES 1:17

Kids love presents! Grown-ups do, too.
Christmas is a time for giving and getting presents. Wrapped packages under Christmas trees
hold all kinds of surprises. What could be inside? Maybe a doll, a truck, a game, pajamas, or
even underwear! Stockings hang stuffed with
little gifts like candy, a toothbrush, a book, or
crayons.

People give presents at Christmas to remember that the wise men brought gifts to Baby Jesus. The wise men brought expensive gifts fit
for a king. But Christmas gifts do not have to
be expensive. The best gifts might surprise you

because they do not come in boxes wrapped in brightly colored paper.

Spending time together, making someone happy, being gentle and kind, sharing, and being patient—all of these are gifts of love, and love is the best gift of all.

The Bible says that God is love. Because God loved people so much, He gave them Jesus. And Jesus loved people so much that He made a way for them to live forever in heaven.

"Thank You, God, for Your gifts of love!"

Dear Father, thank You for Christmas presents, but most of all thank You for love.

The Twelve Days of Christmas

On the twelfth day of Christmas,
My true love sent to me
Twelve lords a-leaping,
Eleven ladies dancing,
Ten pipers piping,
Nine drummers drumming,
Eight maids a-milking,

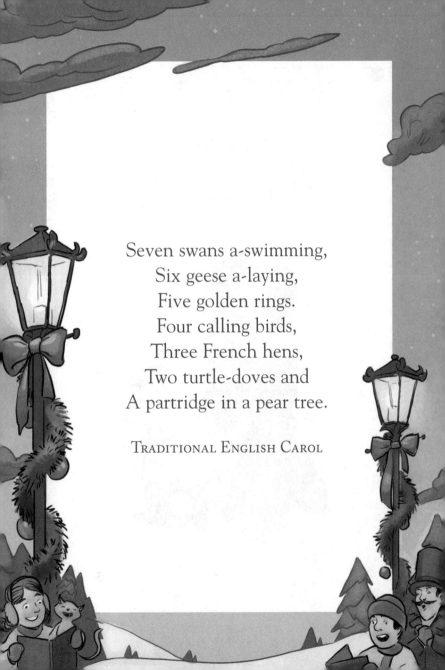

Seven swans a-swimming,
Six geese a-laying,
Five golden rings.
Four calling birds,
Three French hens,
Two turtle-doves and
A partridge in a pear tree.

TRADITIONAL ENGLISH CAROL

The Best Gift of All

Evening, and morning, and at noon,
will I pray, and cry aloud:
and he shall hear my voice.

PSALM 55:17

NOW you know all about Christmas. You know that God loves His people. He made a promise, and He kept it. He sent His Son, Jesus, into the world as a baby, and everything that God planned happened. Jesus grew up, and He made a way for people to get to heaven some day—but that is another story for another time.

Christmas is Jesus' birthday. It is a time to have fun and celebrate. But, even more, it is a time to remember and thank God for Jesus.

Praying is talking to God. You can talk with Him all the time because God loves hearing your prayers. You can pray to tell God what is going on in your life. You can ask Him for something for yourself or for others. And you can tell Him "thank You."

Thank God for His blessings. Thank Him for your family and friends. Thank Him for loving you and watching over you. And especially thank God for giving you the best Christmas present of all—Jesus!

(Tonight, make up your own
bedtime prayer. Tell God some
of the things you have learned
about Christmas.)

HERE WE COME A-CAROLING
(REPRISE)

God bless the Master of this house,
Likewise the Mistress, too
And all the little children,
That round the table go.

Chorus:
Love and joy come to you,
And to your carol, too,
And God bless you and send you
a happy New Year,
And God send you
a happy New Year.

TRADITIONAL ENGLISH CAROL

About the Author

Jean Fischer's writing career began in the 1980s when she worked as an editor for a leading children's book publisher. Today, she writes full time. Jean has written many Christian books for adults and children, including several fiction books in Barbour's *Camp Club Girls* series. Home is Racine, Wisconsin, where she enjoys the beauty of Lake Michigan, woodland wildlife, and her backyard gardens.